CONTENTS

INTRODUCTION

A BRIEF HISTORY OF ORMOND CASTLE

ORMOND CASTLE, CARRICK ON SUIR, is situated at a strategic position on the river Suir, commanding access to the important town of Clonmel to the north and the busy port of Waterford to the south. Carrick's significance in the 16th century can be measured by its inclusion under its old name of Carrickmacgriffin on Boazio's famous map of Ireland, dedicated to Queen Elizabeth in 1599.

The Castle takes its name from its former owners, the powerful Anglo-Norman family of Butler, who came to Ireland in 1171, and became Earls of Ormond, later Dukes of Ormonde (the Dukedom is spelt with an 'e'). James Butler (d.1338) was created 1st Earl of Ormond and married Eleanor of Bohun, granddaughter of Edward II, the king of England who had granted lands and the manor of Carrick to his father, Edmund Butler, in 1315.

Above: a view of the castle at night

Ormond Castle was built between the 14th and 16th centuries. The walls enclosing the site run down to the river and form part of the earlier Ormond castle; the two tall towers standing behind the north range were probably built during the 15th century. Thomas Butler, 10th Earl of Ormond, commenced building this new north range, or manor house as it is commonly referred to, at Carrick during the 1560s. His descendants lived there for well over a hundred years until the last quarter of the 17th century. Ormond Castle was then let to various tenants but remained in the ownership of the Butler family until the 20th century. The castle is now a national monument in the ownership of the Office of Public Works, on behalf of the State.

Below: the principal facade of the north range.

THE APPROACH

Today the principal front of the castle faces northwards onto the remnants of its once great park. Originally there would have been outbuildings such as a gate-house, stable blocks and lodge, with gardens and orchards to the west of the castle. The north range forms a half H-shaped house of two stories with attic space, just one room deep. There is a long central block and two projecting wings abutting the two earlier tall towers to the south. On the symmetrical northern front there are three bays to either side of a projecting central bay, which also contains the principal entrance to the manor house. The exterior of the building is very plain, the only decoration being hood-mouldings over the windows which have curved heads of semi-elliptical shape and rising gables topped by ornamental finials. There are two large bay windows, one on the north front, the other on the east side at the junction with the tower. All of the windows have stone mullions and would have originally been glazed with small leaded panes of glass. Although the bare rubble stonework looks charming to the modern eye, the building would have been coated with a plaster render and whitewashed on the exterior and interior court walls. The modest facade belies the richness of the interior decoration of this house.

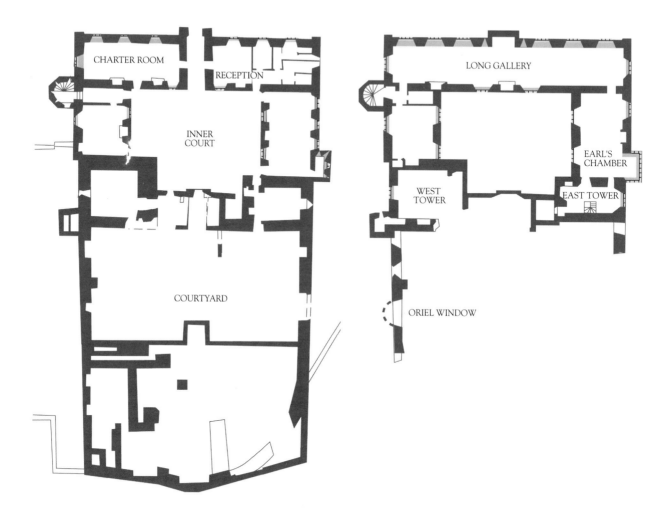

CHARTER ROOM

RECEPTION

INNER
COURT

COURTYARD

Ground Floor Plan

LONG GALLERY

EARL'S
CHAMBER

WEST
TOWER

EAST TOWER

ORIEL WINDOW

First Floor Plan

A Short Tour of the Castle

To either side of the entrance there are gun loops, a reminder of the defensive nature of Irish buildings of this period. Portraits of the 10th Earl of Ormond and of Queen Elizabeth I of England, painted a fresco, face one another over the doors in the entrance passage. When the north range was built, rooms on the ground floor would have consisted of a hall, parlours and lodgings, where visitors and senior members of the Earl of Ormond's household ate and had their accommodation. The hall in post-medieval houses was mainly used by the servants as a dining room and as a place where they gathered when not occupied with tasks.

Left: entrance is made through an arched doorway in the principal facade of the north range.

Above: King Charles II of England (1630 -1685), detail of head from charter in Ormond Castle collection.

Right: inner court. Such courts were a feature of houses built during the 16th century in Ireland and England. Originally a defensive feature their main purpose was to supply light when exterior walls had narrow slit windows at ground level. The north range at Ormond Castle had much narrower windows at ground level on the frontage when it was built.

Ground Floor

Rooms on the ground floor to the east (left) of the entrance lobby are now used by OPW for the reception area and other offices. Some of these rooms may have had decorative plasterwork and other features which have been lost over the centuries.

■ Room 1

A large undecorated room with an interesting limestone fireplace bearing a dual coat of arms and the date 1641 incised on it. The arms depicted are those of James Butler (1610-1688), then Earl of Ormond (later first Duke of Ormonde) and those of his wife Lady Elizabeth Preston (c. 1615-1684), Baroness Dingwall.

■ Room 11 The Charter Room

This room houses an interesting collection of Royal Charters granted to various members of the Butler family. The earliest charters date back to Charles II (1630-1685) and these can be easily identified by the King's portrait seen in miniature above the text. Others bear portraits of King William III (1650-1702) and Queen Mary II (1662-1694), who were joint rulers, of William III on his own and of Queen Anne (1665 -1714), Mary's sister, and the last Stuart monarch to sit on the English throne.
On the left hand wall are two fireplaces and a doorway giving access to the inner court. It is likely that this room was originally used as the hall of the newly built north range.

☐ Inner Court

A small courtyard such as this, typical in 16th century buildings, was commonplace in England. The Rothe House in Kilkenny, of slightly later date, has similar courtyards. The

walls of the house which form its sides would have been rendered and probably whitewashed with a lime wash. A cut stone gateway decorated with well defined mouldings and a carved shield displaying the Chief Indented, an early form of the Butler arms, probably those

of James Butler, 9th Earl of Ormond (d. 1546), is on the south side of the court, inserted into the remains of a wall between the two 15th century towers. The tower on the left (east) is slightly smaller and earlier. Both of these towers were integrated with the new north range when it was first built and the remains of connecting doorways at a number of levels can be seen in the walls of both towers.

◼ Room III The New Parlour

Entrance to this room is through the doorway on the western side of the court. During the late 16th and throughout the 17th centuries, parlours such as this were often used by the family for informal dining. In a large household such as that of the 10th Earl of Ormond, it may have been where the upper servants, or at least the gentlewomen, retired to have meals. It is probable that this room was additional to earlier parlours elsewhere in the complex of buildings which previously existed in the lower courtyard.

The furnishings of such a room in the 16th century would have been quite sparse. A folding table, some chairs, perhaps a sideboard and few other pieces of furniture would have been sufficient. There would have been curtains for the windows and covers for some of the furniture. In a room for dining such as this, the walls would have had wainscot (panelling) below the frieze, while the floor may have had coverings of plaited rushwork.

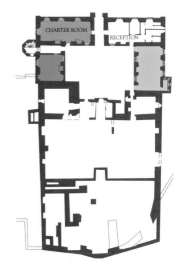

Above: a carved wooden bed dated 1606.

The Decorative Plasterwork. The decorated plaster frieze which remains on just two walls of this room would, of course, have continued around all four. The ceiling is not original and may have been decorated. Some of the frieze is missing and what remains is divided by plain mouldings into simple compartments, within which are heraldic devices or badges of the Butler/Ormond family. Two heraldic beasts, the griffin and the falcon, supporters of the Ormond arms, alternate with an Ormond, or Wake, knot (in Ireland this is called a Carrick knot). The plasterwork overmantel is also divided into compartments, one containing the Butler arms showing the Chief Indented quartered with three covered cups, and the other a crest (a falcon rising out of plumes) with the initials T.O. for Thomas Ormond and the Butler family motto *Comme Je Trouve*. Both of these armorial devices are superimposed on fashionable strapwork backgrounds; small strapwork motifs also feature at each corner. This type of decoration would probably have been painted in bright heraldic colours.

■ The Staircase

A modern concrete staircase is housed in an angular tower. The area at the bottom of the staircase contained a doorway which gave access to the gardens.

It is unlikely that this staircase formed the principal route to the state rooms on the first floor. A more elaborate staircase within some of the earlier buildings probably gave access to the old great chamber in the south west tower. From there important visitors could proceed along the sequence of state rooms on the first floor.

First Floor

The State Rooms

Post-medieval houses often featured such state rooms – a suite of richly decorated 'best rooms,' designed to receive important visitors and to demonstrate their owner's wealth and status. It is probable that Thomas Butler added the north range to the original structures at Ormond Castle for this very reason. The suite would usually consist of a great chamber, withdrawing chamber, bedroom, adjacent closets and a long gallery nearby. The state rooms at Ormond castle were situated on the first floor of the newly built north range and were integrated with rooms on a corresponding level in the two towers. The following sequence is suggested for the 16th century state rooms in this building. It is based on early 17th century Butler family inventories of Kilkenny Castle where the 10th Earl had also built a new north range: in the west tower (old building) first floor – the great chamber (now ruined); adjoining it in the north range – room V, the new dining chamber; then room VI, the long gallery; room VII, the Earl's chamber; finally, in the east tower (old building) – room VIII, the withdrawing chamber.

■ Room V The New Dining Chamber

This room has rich plasterwork decoration, appropriate to its position on the principal floor of the house. It would have been the second in a sequence of state rooms, between the adjoining great chamber in the now ruined west tower and the long gallery. The armorial nature of the plaster decoration would suggest the function of the room was a public one, such as a dining chamber, rather than a withdrawing room or best bedroom.

In the 16th century such an important room would have had tapestries on the walls, hanging below the painted plasterwork frieze. Furnishings might also have included folding tables covered with table carpets and some chairs and footstools, with richly fringed curtains at the windows, while candles in gilt candlesticks provided lighting.

Decorative Plasterwork. It can be seen at a glance that the plasterwork frieze in this room is more elaborate than that in the parlour downstairs. It displays the Butler arms and crest motifs, which alternate within panels set between borders of guilloche ornament with small lion masks at each junction. Over the limestone fireplace with plain mouldings are the Butler arms executed in plaster, supported by a griffin and falcon and bearing an elaborate falcon crest with initials T.O. These arms are quartered with those of the Earls of Carrick and Desmond. An armorial decorative scheme such as this, proclaiming the family titles, would have been deemed suitable for a dining chamber, and painted in bright colours. The ceiling in this room was partially intact and has been restored to its original form with decorative plaster mouldings, foliage ornament and pendants arranged in geometric compartments.

The Small Closet. A closet would have existed in the space between the two rooms. Closets were small rooms for private use often well decorated and furnished with writing chest or table and some chairs. Such closets were often situated close to chimney breasts as was this example.

◼ Room VI The Long Gallery

This is the earliest and finest example of a long gallery remaining in Ireland. Originating in Italy and France, long galleries of this type became very fashionable in England after 1550. Prior to this date galleries were quite modest and in some cases derived from covered access in courtyard houses. Usually the longest room in the house, they were commonly used for indoor exercise and from their position on the upper floors could command a view of the surrounding park and gardens. Eventually they were integrated into the State Rooms and, as in this example, often adjoined the owner's private chambers. At Ormond Castle the long gallery was created for ostentatious display, hence the elaborate plasterwork and fireplaces. It was also used as a visual demonstration of the earl's loyalty to, and links with, the Tudor monarchy, particularly the Queen, Elizabeth I and her brother, King Edward VI.

In the 16th century, long galleries were often sparsely furnished. The walls of the gallery here were probably covered below the decorative frieze with wainscot (panelling), which may have been painted. Tapestries were often displayed in important galleries such as this, hanging, probably, along the inner fireplace wall. Portrait collections were a usual feature of a gallery, designed to impress the visitor with pictures of family members, friends, ancestors, kings, queens and other powerful patrons and connections.

Above: the plasterwork overmantel in the long gallery, displaying the portrait of Elizabeth I between the figures of Iustacia and Equitas on the upper tier and the Tudor Royal arms between two fashionable strapwork cartouches on the lower tier.

Right: the long gallery looking west.

Fireplaces and Plasterwork. There are two fireplaces in this long room. The great stone fireplace is undoubtedly an Irish piece and in its execution displays an impressive

virility which contrasts strongly with the restrained plaster example further down the room. Here again the full Butler arms with supporting male griffins are displayed but on this occasion they are in an unusual form. Instead of a normal quartering, there are repetitions of the Chief Indented and the covered cups of the

Butlers with the Desmond arms. The Wake, or Carrick, knot is also repeated four times, between the legs of the griffins and at the upper corners above the flowing plumes. The Latin inscription reads as follows:

above,
ANNO.DNI.1565.ANNO.REGNI.REGINE.ELIZABETH.SEPTIMO.

below,
THOMAS.BUTLER.MILES.VICOMES.DE.TURLES.COMES.
ORMONDIE.ET.OSSORIE.DNS.LIBERTATIS.SEV.REGALITATIS.
COMITATUS.TIPPARE.AC.DNS.THESAURAE.REGNI.HIBNE.ME.
FIERI.FECIT.

"In the year of Our Lord 1565, the seventh year of the reign of Queen Elizabeth
Thomas Butler. Knight Viscount Thurles Earl of Ormond and Ossory
.......had me made."

The supporting pedestals are decorated with vaulting patterns very similar in scale and execution to those found on the stone baptismal font at Kilcooley Abbey.

Above: the figure of Iusticia (Justice) is shown holding the hilt of a sword in her right hand.

Left: the great stone fireplace in the long gallery. This piece was probably carved by members of the local O'Tunney sculpture workshop.

During the late 19th century this fireplace was removed and taken to Kilkenny Castle. It was brought back and reinstated here in the 1970's.

Decorative Plasterwork. Further down the gallery above the second fireplace, there is a plasterwork overmantel which has two tiers of decoration, each divided into three panels by plain plaster mouldings. In the central compartment of the lower tier are displayed the armorial bearings of England and France surmounted by the royal crown and supported by the lion and dragon of the Tudors. On either side are elaborate strapwork motifs. In the upper tier is a portrait bust of Queen Elizabeth I of England, encircled by a laurel wreath within a square frame. At each corner of the frame are small mythical beasts (dragons)

Above: the figure of Equitas (Equity) is shown holding scales in her left hand.

Above Right: drawing of Queen Elizabeth's monogram from ceiling.

Right: long gallery ceiling detail, showing the Tudor Royal arms and various other Tudor badges, such as the portcullis, Tudor rose, fleur-de-lys and Queen Elizabeth's monogram.

holding fleur-de-lys. To either side of the central panel, standing in moulded aedicules with their names suspended above their heads, are classically draped figures representing Justice (Iustacia) and Equity (Equestas). Justice was a favoured symbol of the period, and was often depicted as the Goddess Astrea, which was one of the Queen's favourite conceits. Iustacia is usually depicted with scales in one hand and sword in the other. Equestas also holds a pair of scales in her hand and sometimes is shown with a plummet in the other. This trio of motifs, together with the arms of Queen Elizabeth I, are repeated in the rich plasterwork frieze that runs around the long gallery. The motifs are divided by moulded fluted pilasters supported on delicately designed brackets. A second portrait bust of the young King Edward VI also features in the decoration of this room. The scheme is cleverly arranged so that the portraits of Edward and Elizabeth alternate and face one another across the room. This can be seen most clearly at the plasterwork fireplace which is opposite the alcove.

The ceiling is very richly decorated. On it can be seen the Royal arms, the Queen's monogram and various Tudor badges – the rose, chained portcullis and fleur-de-lys. Straight moulded plaster ribs divide the whole area into geometric compartments, with plaster pendants surrounded by decorative foliage intersecting at regular intervals. The principal shape is the square which contains the Royal arms; each is surrounded by lozenges which also frame the other badges.

The plaster overmantel in this room has survived almost intact, but portions of the ceiling and frieze were badly damaged and have had to be restored and reconstructed.

Left: the panelling in this room was removed to Kilkenny Castle and has recently been returned and reinstated.

Room VII The New Great Chamber - The Earl's Chamber

This large room would probably have served a dual purpose, both as the principal room and as the 10th Earl's chamber. A small closet would have adjoined this room. The deeply recessed window is typical of the period; it is an important feature and provided space for private conversation apart from the rest of the company.

In the 16th century such an important room would have been furnished with richly upholstered chairs and footstools, folding tables, some rugs on the floor and elaborate curtains at the windows, with fine tapestries on the walls. At a later date, possibly during the 18th century, this room had been fitted with wooden panelling, which was taken out and placed in Kilkenny Castle during the late 19th century. This panelling has since been brought back and reinstated in the room.

Decorative Plasterwork. The plasterwork frieze in this room contains the largest proportion of original decorative plasterwork remaining in the house. It is of a very high standard in both ornament and technical quality and some of the panels display an element of sophistication not found in any of the other rooms. The frieze around the room features a series of panels of various types, some of which bear motifs found

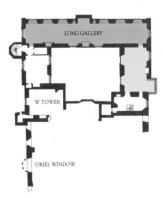

Right: the Earl's chamber, showing detail from plasterwork frieze, a decorative strapwork cartouche with the words plues pense que e dere, *'to think rather than to speak'. These words written in old French are taken from a poem 'Le Tourment Cache', (The Hidden Torment), written by the poet Charles d'Orleans (1394-1465).*

Below: the Earl's chamber, showing detail from plasterwork frieze, the arms of the Butler family, the Chief Indented and three covered cups of the Butlers quartered with the arms of the Earl of Carrick and the arms of Desmond, with supporters of falcon and griffin, surmounted by a crest with falcon rising from a plume of feathers.

elsewhere in the state apartments. Plasterworkers have obviously made use of the same moulds for the elaborate strapwork motifs found also on the lower tier of the plaster overmantel in the long gallery and for the Butler family arms from the dining chamber. Finely wrought strapwork panels of a more delicate nature, decorated with elfin creatures, masks, rings and loops, alternate with others containing the motto 'plues pense que e dere' and with panels displaying the Butler arms, also reproduced in other rooms. Elongated, elegant caryatids in a mannerist style separate the frieze panels. The ceiling, which is quite plain with restrained mouldings forming geometric patterns, has been restored. No trace of an overmantel has been found, which suggests that it was made of plaster, a more fragile material than stone.

■ Room VIII The Withdrawing Chamber

This room is situated in the east tower and was integrated with the first floor rooms of the north range during the 16th century. It may have been here that the withdrawing chamber was situated.

Today, a wooden staircase has been erected to give access to the attic storey above. Previously the mural stairs in the thickness of the walls would have been used to gain access to the room above this one.

The Tower Room

This room shows signs of extensive reconstruction and gives few clues to its previous function. Of interest is the arched stone recess in the north wall of the room with its carved example of foliage ornament visible on the central section. Two carved stone angels and scrolls can be seen just above the springing of the arch. These may be compared with other examples of carved angels found at Granagh Castle and more particularly with those on the tomb of Piers Butler, 8th Earl of Ormond, and his wife, Margaret FitzGerald, in St Canice's Cathedral in Kilkenny. It would seem most likely that this room retains its form from the time of the 8th Earl's residence at the castle and that the decorative angels also date from this period.

Above: the eastern tower one of two carved angels from the upper room.

Left: the mural stairs in the thickness of the eastern tower wall.

Below: eastern tower, detail of arched structure showing carved foliage design. Access to the tower room is by a mural staircase from the second floor of the east tower.

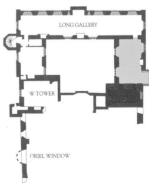

Right: the 16th century roof retains
most of its original timbers. It is a
simple oak truss roof, constructed
with the use of timber joints and
dowels or pegs, without any nails
or other fixings.

The Attic Storey

This is the second floor of the north range. The rooms at this level, which have double light windows, would have provided lodgings for many of the servants in the 16th century. Large storage spaces or wardrobes for holding spare furniture, carpets, beds and changes of soft furnishings for summer and winter might also have been housed up here.

Today, access to the attic space allows the visitor to inspect and appreciate the intricate structure of the timber structures supporting the roof.

THE BUTLER FAMILY

THE BUTLERS WERE one of the most important families of Anglo-Norman origin in Ireland. They were descended from Theobald Walter (d.1206) who came to Ireland in 1171. Theobald was a successful and resourceful man who found in Ireland a suitable arena for his many talents. He obtained lands in this country and was granted *prisage* on the import of wines by the king. He was also given the title of Chief Butler of Ireland from which the family name derives. During the 13th and 14th centuries the family continued to advance in prosperity and power, acquiring more lands and titles. In 1315 Edmund FitzWalter (1290-1321), 6th Chief Butler, was granted the Lordship and Manor of Carrick by King Edward II. His son James (d. 1338), now known by the surname Butler, was created 1st Earl of Ormond and made an advantageous marriage to Eleanor de Bohun, granddaughter of King Edward II of England. By the 15th century the Butlers owned huge tracts of land mainly centred on the present day counties of Kilkenny, and Tipperary. The 3rd Earl of Ormond, another James (d.1405), also acquired the strong castle at Kilkenny from the powerful Marshall family, descendants of the Earl of Pembroke. The FitzGeralds, Earls of Desmond and also of Anglo-Norman origin, held

Above: stone carving displaying the Chief Indented, an early form of Butler arms, inserted over the gateway in the inner court.

Above: James Butler, (d. 1546), 9th Earl of Ormond also identified as Thomas Boleyn, Earl of Wiltshire, drawing by Hans Holbein the Younger (1497/8-1543).

lands to the west and north of the Butler holdings and were their main rivals for control of the southern half of the country. Despite frequent intermarriage, disputes between these two families continued over the centuries from generation to generation.

Between the years 1452 and 1515, three sons of the 4th Earl of Ormond succeeded to the title. All three of them are known to have been absent from Ireland for long periods. John Butler (d.1478), 6th Earl, went on a mission to Portugal in 1472 and his brother Thomas Butler (d. 1515), 7th Earl, spent the years from 1505 to 1515 in England. While there, the 7th Earl was granted a fine manor house at Beaulieu in Essex by King Henry VII. He entertained Henry VIII there in 1510 and again in 1515. On his death this English property went to his daughter, Margaret, who had married William Boleyn. A generation later this marriage was to be the cause of a serious dispute over the Earldom of Ormond. Because the 7th Earl had no direct male heir, King Henry VIII had in 1527 granted the title to Thomas Boleyn, father of his queen, the famous Anne. However, Piers Ruadh Butler (c. 1467-1539), a descendant of James Butler, 3rd Earl, was successful in regaining the title in 1538 and became 8th Earl. He had also been granted the Earldom of Ossory in 1528.

Piers had married Margaret FitzGerald, daughter of the 8th Earl of Kildare in c. 1485. This couple were great builders. They are credited with important additions to Granagh Castle in Co. Kilkenny, they rebuilt another Butler castle at Gowran, Co. Kilkenny, founded Kilkenny College in 1536 and they were also responsible for work at Ormond Castle.

In 1539, Piers was succeeded by his son, James Butler, 9th Earl of Ormond (d. 1546), who had been created Viscount Thurles in 1536. James had married Joan FitzGerald, daughter of the 11th Earl of Desmond. It was their son, Thomas Butler (1531-1614), 10th Earl of Ormond, Earl of Ossory and Viscount Thurles, known as 'Black Tom', who built the new north range at Carrick. Piers Butler, his son James and his grandson Thomas had all attended at the English court and were familiar with current trends and new ideas circulating at that time. The advent of the Reformation and the subsequent suppression and dissolution of religious houses resulted in a very considerable increase in the size and wealth of Butler landholdings.

THOMAS BUTLER, 10TH EARL OF ORMOND (1531-1614)

Thomas Butler, Earl of Ossory and 10th Earl of Ormond succeeded to his titles and lands in 1546 at the early age of fifteen, at a time of momentous historical events in Ireland and England. Under the Tudors the renewed conquest of Ireland had begun. Henry VIII, whose title had been Lord of Ireland, had himself declared King of Ireland in 1541. Many of the Gaelic lordships were won over and had their lands granted back to them by the Crown. The dismantling of some of the powerful Anglo-Norman lordships was taking place following the defeat of the FitzGeralds, Earls of Kildare. Colonization was being introduced in a more methodical way. To complicate matters further, the Reformation was in full swing in England and by the beginning of the following century the Protestant church had consolidated itself in law. This meant that it was also to be the official religion of Ireland, an issue which was to be the cause of divisiveness and complications in the relationship between the two countries for centuries to come.

Thomas Butler had been away from Ireland from an early age; his boyhood upbringing was at the English court where he shared a tutor with the future king, Edward VI. Thomas was present at Edward's coronation in 1546, when he was also installed as a Knight of the Order of the Bath. After the death of the young king, he remained at court and continued to prosper during the reign of the Catholic Queen Mary. When her sister, Elizabeth, who was also Thomas's distant cousin through the Boleyns, ascended the throne in 1558, he continued to enjoy royal favour and was appointed to the lucrative post of Lord Treasurer of Ireland the following year.

On his return to Ireland after this first long sojourn at court, the young Thomas was considered 'wholly English' by those in power in England, in contrast to the FitzGeralds of Desmond who were considered to be 'Irish' and therefore not to be trusted. Ormond was to continue to prove his loyalty to the Crown in the matter of Irish affairs during his lifetime. While doing so he seems also to have retained some measure of good will with the Gaelic Irish.

Above: Thomas Butler, (1531-1614), 10th Earl of Ormond, portrait, oil on panel by an unknown artist.

Above: capture of Thomas Earl of Ormond by O'More 1600. (Reproduced with permission of Trinity College Library Dublin Manuscripts Department, MS. 1208/13). In April 1600 Thomas Earl of Ormond accompanied by Sir George Carew and Donogh O'Brien, Earl of Thomond set out to parley with Owny Mac Rory O'More. The Earl of Ormond was captured and held prisoner by the O'Mores.

In 1562, the 10th Earl was in Ireland fighting the 'outlaws of Leix' for the Queen. Two years later a battle was fought at Affane, Co. Kilkenny between the FitzGeralds of Desmond and the Butlers of Ormond, this time over rival claims to land in west Waterford. The struggle between these two families continued for five years and incurred the Queen's severe displeasure at such discord between two of her most powerful subjects in Ireland. In June 1565 Elizabeth expressed her anger with Ormond. He replied in a petition dated September of that year, formally submitting to the Queen and stating that 'He will never stand in law against his dread sovereign lady' but 'humbly submits'. He was to prove his loyalty to her by his suppression of a rebellion led by his own three brothers and James FitzMaurice in 1569. Many favours were lavished on him by a grateful monarch throughout her long reign. He was installed as a Knight of the Garter in 1588 and carried the Sword of State before the Queen at the Tilbury review held to celebrate victory over the Spanish Armada. Thomas Butler's preferential position in Ireland was confirmed by his many offices in this country. He was Lord President of Munster, Lord High Mareschal of Ireland and Commander in Chief of Her Majesty's forces in Ireland. The years between 1569 and 1582 seem to have been relatively peaceful until the final phase in the struggle with the Earl of Desmond began in 1582; this resulted in FitzGerald's being hunted down, his subsequent death and the final eclipse of that family's power in Ireland.

This period also seems to have been the time when Ormond's standing at Court was at its highest. His name features frequently in the New Year lists of gifts given and received by the Queen. At New Year 1577-78 Ormond presented the Queen with a jewel described as 'a fair jewel of gold being a phenix, the wings fully garnished with rubies etc.' Ten years later the Queen presented Ormond with a gold George of the Order of the Garter and in the same year at the christening of his daughter Elizabeth, the Queen's gift to mark the occasion was a silver gilt basin and ewer.

Towards the end of the sixteenth century the 10th Earl of Ormond was also involved in political negotiations on behalf of the Queen with Hugh O'Neill, Earl of Tyrone, the greatest and most powerful of the Gaelic Irish leaders. However, this did not spare him the indignity of being captured by the O'Mores in 1600.

Much has been made of the Irishness of the Anglo-Norman Lords. It is known, however, that the Ormond branch of the Butler family had maintained very strong links with the English court for several generations before the 10th Earl. Thomas Butler was seen as a loyal servant of the Crown in Ireland where his knowledge of the land and his contacts with both Norman Irish and Gaelic Irish were to prove useful for those whose principal aim was the subjugation and colonization of that country. After a lifetime spent in service to the English Crown, however, his relations with the Court seem to have soured. When he retired to Carrick in his last years, he was almost blind and suffering from attacks of ague.

Although he had married three times, Thomas Butler outlived all his legitimate male heirs. He married as his first wife, Elizabeth, daughter of 6th Lord Berkely in 1559 and divorced her in 1563. His second marriage to Elizabeth (d.1600), daughter of John, 2nd Baron Sheffield, produced, in 1583, a male heir who died when he was only six years old. Finally, Helen, daughter of 3rd Viscount Buttevant, and widow of one John Power, became his third wife in 1601. Because he had no surviving male heir, all of his properties were inherited by his daughter Elizabeth (d.1628), while his titles went to a nephew, Walter Butler (d.1632), a member of the Kilcash branch of the Butler family, who became 11th Earl of Ormond. Thomas Butler died in 1614 at the age of eighty-three at Ormond Castle, his favourite home in his old age. He was buried under a handsome monument (since destroyed) sculpted by Nicholas Stone in St. Canice's Cathedral in Kilkenny.

Above: James Butler, (1610-1688), 12th Earl of Ormond, Marquess and later 1st Duke of Ormonde. The sitter is shown holding a baton of command, Ormond was Commander in Chief of the King's army in Ireland. This portrait was painted by Sir Peter Lely (1618-80), in 1647 when Ormond went to Oxford to visit the king, Charles I for the last time.

ORMOND CASTLE AFTER THOMAS 10TH EARL OF ORMOND

One of Thomas Butler's last letters written from Carrick in 1613 was addressed to his daughter Elizabeth, sympathising with her on the death of her first husband, Theobald Butler, Viscount Tulleophelim. Elizabeth and her husband had been living at Kilkenny when he died but we know from letters written by that couple from Carrick that they also lived at Ormond Castle. When Thomas died at Ormond Castle in 1614, leaving no male heir, it was to cause a further series of disputes over land and titles within the family. Eventually the lands were granted by the English King James I to Richard Preston, created Earl of Desmond, the second husband of Elizabeth, daughter of Thomas, the 10th Earl,

Left: rubbing from coat of arms inscribed on stone fireplace in a ground floor room in Ormond Castle. The coats of arms are those of the 12th Earl of Ormond and his wife Elizabeth Preston, Baroness Dingwall, with the date 1641.

Above: detail from portrait of Elizabeth Preston (c.1616-84), Baroness Dingwall, wife of James 12th Earl (later 1st Duke of Ormonde), attributed to David des Granges, (1611-c.1671/72).

and heir to his properties. The problems caused by her second marriage were solved when her own daughter, Elizabeth, married a cousin, James Butler (1610-1688) Viscount Thurles, in 1629. The marriage of this young couple reunited the lands and titles of the Ormond family.

This James Butler, who had married Elizabeth, granddaughter of the 10th Earl, was the grandson of Walter, 11th Earl of Ormond. Walter also lived at Ormond Castle and in 1630, James Butler, then Lord Thurles, brought his young bride to live there with his grandparents. Two years later Earl Walter died there and the young couple continued to live at the castle for a few more years. A fireplace on the ground floor has a fine incised display of both their coats of arms bearing the date 1641. That was also the year in which the Countess Elizabeth had to leave Carrick and move with her young family to Dublin following the outbreak of rebellion. James, by that time 12th Earl of Ormond, was a staunch royalist throughout the difficult years of the English civil war, having been appointed Commander-in-Chief of the King's Army in Ireland. He was at Ormond Castle prior to the attack on it by Cromwell in 1649. In 1650 he fled to France and travelled about Europe with the exiled King Charles II until 1660. For his loyal service James had been created Marquess of Ormonde in 1642 and was elevated to the Dukedom of Ormonde on the Restoration of King Charles II to the throne in 1660. How seriously Ormond Castle was damaged during the Cromwellian attack and seizure is not known. It must have been fairly extensive because in 1661 Elizabeth, then Duchess of Ormonde, wrote to her agent that 'the house at Carrick is in a ruinous condition'.

James Butler, Duke of Ormonde, like many of his ancestors, had been educated in England. He was a solid statesman and was appointed the King's Viceroy, Lord Lieutenant of Ireland, for three terms. He divided his time between England and Ireland, moving freely between the two countries. Kilkenny Castle was the principal seat of the family in Ireland, while Dunmore House in Co. Kilkenny was the Duchess of Ormonde's favourite residence. Viceregal accommodation was at Dublin Castle and the Phoenix near Chapelizod, now the Phoenix Park. Although the Duke and Duchess had lived at Ormond Castle during the 1630s and '40s, they did not reside there after their return to Ireland in 1661. They had several houses in England, including Ormond House in St. James's Square, London, and Moor Park, Hertfordshire. In their later days the Duke and Duchess of Ormonde had as their country reatreat, Kingston Hall (Kingston Lacey) in Dorset, England.

When the ducal couple returned to Ireland after the Restoration in 1661 their attention was focused on restoring and rebuilding Kilkenny Castle and Dunmore House. A major building programme that was to continue for over twenty years was begun at Kilkenny, while the refurbishment of Dunmore House does not seem to have been completed before that house was abandoned when the Duchess died in 1684. A telling omission which points towards the eventual fate of Ormond Castle was the failure to initiate any major rebuilding programme there or to install a water supply during the years 1669-70 when those projects were being carried out at both Kilkenny and Dunmore. The Duchess's correspondence of the period contains a few desultory enquiries about the state of Ormond Castle and instructions to ensure that 'it is kept dry' but no mention of any large scale repairs. The Duke kept his stable there and occasionally visited to inspect his horses. In 1668, he wrote, 'My Lord Glenawley tells me some disease is gotten into my stable at Carrick where the hopefullest colts and fillys are'. He was also interested in the maintenance of his deer park there. The Duke and Duchess continued to refer to Ormond Castle at Carrick in their letters throughout the rest of their lives. They wrote to their agents at various times enquiring about the peach house, orchards, gardens, deer park, pigeon house and warrens there. A letter from the Duke at Carrick is dated 1679, but he does not seem to have returned there after that date.

Above: James Butler, (1610-1688), 1st Duke of Ormonde. This portrait was painted in 1662 by Sir Peter Lely (1618-80), after the restoration of Charles II to the throne. Ormond is depicted wearing robes of the order of the garter. In his right hand he holds the wand of office of Lord Steward of the King's household.

TENANTS IN THE 17TH CENTURY

By 1669 the Duke of Ormonde was writing letters about installing his old friend, Sir Ralph Freeman and his wife as tenants at Ormond Castle. Also in that year Ormonde mentioned a number of French merchant families that he was keen to install at the castle. The arrangement does not seem to have been a happy one as Sir Ralph wrote to him frequently, complaining about the noise created by the French families who were sharing the premises with him. A number of alterations to the house may have been

made at this time in order to accommodate the different households living there. A range of ovens in the courtyard were found to be still in situ as late as 1950.

JAMES BUTLER
2ND DUKE OF ORMONDE

BY 1743, the house at Carrick is described in the following terms 'Here are the ruins of a fine old house that did belong to the late Duke of Ormond'. James, 1st Duke of Ormonde was succeeded by his grandson, James Butler (1665-1745), as 2nd Duke. Although he was a hero of the Battle of the Boyne, fighting on the side of King William III, the Duke was to side with the Stuart cause and was attainted for his Jacobite sympathies in 1716. He spent most of the remainder of his life in exile in Avignon and was granted a pension from the Spanish government. With nobody apparently at the helm, the Ormond properties in Ireland were allowed to fall into decay. The 2nd Duke's brother, Charles, Earl of Arran (1671-1758), had inherited the titles but he never visited Ireland after 1716 and when he died childless the Dukedom and Marquessate of Ormonde became extinct. Walter Butler of Garryricken, a member of the Kilcash branch of the family, claimed to be de jure 16th Earl of Ormond. The title was eventually restored to his cousin, John Butler (1740-95), who was confirmed as the 17th Earl in 1791. John's son, Walter Butler (1770-1820), 18th Earl of Ormond, was created Marquess of Ormond (2nd creation).

Above: James Butler (1665-1745), 2nd Duke of Ormonde, grandson of the 1st Duke. This portrait was painted c. 1712 by Michael Dahl (c. 1659-1743). Ormonde is shown in armour, wearing the ribbon of the garter, holding in his right hand the baton of command as Commander-in-Chief of the King's armies.

TENANTS IN THE 18TH AND 19TH CENTURIES

Ormond Castle seems to have been abandoned by the family in the 18th century and it was let to various tenants. A Waterford wine merchant named Galwey lived there in the 1780s. Later, a Mr. Wogan, a solicitor who was appointed Seneschal for the Marquess of Ormond at his Manor Court, was a tenant. Mason's Parochial Survey of Ireland informs us that this man had many of the old buildings levelled soon after 1816 and that he modernised other sections of the Castle to make it more habitable. It may have been during Wogan's tenancy that a wooden staircase was inserted into the long gallery providing alternate access from the ground floor. Mason's account also tells us that there were still some tapestries at Ormond Castle in the early 19th century. These are also referred to by James Graves in his article about tapestries at Kilkenny Castle written in 1852. It seems that one of a suite of six tapestries of the 'History of Samson' which had been at Ormond Castle was at that time at Kilkenny Castle.

The sad dilapidation and neglect of Ormond Castle may be linked to the gradual running down of the town itself and the preference for Kilkenny Castle as the family seat which took place during the 17th and 18th century. After its heyday as a strong defensive and strategic position on an important river was over, the town prospered as a centre for the cloth industry. Arthur Young visited Carrick in the 1780s and described it as 'one of the greatest manufacturing towns in Ireland' and yet just sixty years later in the mid 19th century the town was referred to as 'sad' with 'a deserted falling off appearance'. The Ormond family seem to have abandoned any interest in the town although they still drew rents from it. In contrast to Ormond Castle, throughout the 19th century Kilkenny Castle was restored and redecorated by the Ormonds who continued to live there. At the end of the 19th century, Ormond Castle was occupied by a caretaker and his family who lived there until the 1950s.

Left: Ormond (Carrick) Castle, drawing signed Purcell Pinxit, 1782, view from the south.

THE BUILDINGS OF ORMOND CASTLE

"Here is my Lord of Ormond's house, daintily seated on the river bank, which flows even to the walls of his house, which I went to see, and found in the outer court three or four haystacks, not far from the stable door; this court is paved. There are also two other courts; the one a quadrangle. The house was built at twice." SIR WILLIAM BRERETON. JULY 1635.

To date no building accounts and just one early description of the actual buildings at Ormond Castle have been found. As a result we are left with just the thinnest shreds of written evidence which inform us mainly about dates and the acquisition of lands to the castle. Most of these facts are contained in references to the castle and town of Carrick on Suir which were found in the extensive collection of papers and deeds belonging to the Butler family.

History Of Ormond Castle

Before the north range was built in the 1560s, the two 15th century towers stood within a walled enclosure running down to the river's edge. The castle was situated close to, but probably outside, the town walls. Originally the walled enclosure was D-shaped at the river end where footings of a curved section of wall can still be seen in the eastern corner of the lower courtyard. The ruins of a three-storied watergate still exist on the river frontage and

another gateway building would probably have stood on the northern front. Throughout the centuries buildings within the enclosure were added or altered. The earliest reference to a castle at Carrick is in 1315, when Edmund Butler (d.1321), 6th Butler and Earl of Carrick was granted the castle and manor of Carrickmacgriffin (the medieval name for the town) by King Edward II of England. Later, in

Above: Ormond (Carrick) Castle, 1796. Aquatint, artist Thomas Sautelle Roberts (1760-1826), engraved by J. W. Edy.

Left: Ormond Castle from the river.

Above: Granagh Castle, Co. Kilkenny, (detail) from a drawing by Francis Place (1647-1728) of c. 1690.

1361, James (d. 1382), 2nd Earl of Ormond and his wife Elizabeth obtained the claim of one Bernard de Valle on the town of Carrickmacgriffin. The document verifying this claim contains a written description of the town at that time which delineates its length and breadth. In it the 'Earls Castle' is placed 'on the south, [of the town wall] upon which a chapel and ruin annexed to the said castle are situated'.

Proof exists that there was a habitable castle on the site by 1366. In a deed in which the 2nd Earl is described as being of Ormond and of Carrick, the document is quoted as being given 'in our Castle of Carrick'. However, the building of the existing fortified castle with its towers and walls is traditionally dated to the middle of the following century c.1450 and attributed to Edmund MacRichard Butler (d. 1464), a nephew of James Butler, (d.1452), 4th Earl of Ormond. Earlier references also exist: in 1434 the 4th Earl made arrangements to leave the castle in the care of Annota Walshe, a local woman, and her son Robert. Nine years later, the accounts of the 4th Earl, under the heading of payments made to the Earl of Ormond's servants at Easter term [April 1443], contain a reference to '12 pairs of gloves for the masons of Carrick, 16d'. Other payments to the same masons of 7s. and 13s. 4d are also recorded. It seems that the 4th Earl was having building work carried out at some of his other properties at that time as there are payments made to his workmen at Mellagh (sic) for 'rebuilding the new hall there 19s.1½d' and at Gowran Castle 20s.8d

Thomas Butler (d. 1515), 7th Earl, was in England from 1505 until 1515, during which time he was granted a fine manor house at Beaulieu in Essex by King Henry VII and given permission to crenellate it. At that time the Earls of Ormond also had castles at Kilkenny, Gowran, Knocktopher, Granagh, Carrick and Dunfert in Ireland. While the 7th Earl was away, his kinsman Sir Piers Ruadh Butler (d.1539), acted as Deputy for his Irish lands. It may have been during Piers' stewardship that the larger and later of the two towers at Carrick was erected, as he has recently been credited with the building of a similar five storied tower and a great hall at Granagh Castle, another Butler property in Co. Kilkenny.

Piers' grandson, Thomas Butler (1532-1614) 10th Earl of Ormond, added, c. 1565, a north range and it is this building that makes up the major part of what is known today as Ormond Castle. The dating of this range to 1565 is put forward on the grounds of style of building, patterns of interior decoration, documentary evidence and the presence of this date in three separate sites within the structure. Only a few contemporary references to this house and its grounds have been found. The earliest in 1566 is from a letter written by Sir Thomas Gresham's agent to his master and concerns the purchase of wooden panelling and glass in Antwerp for the Earl of Ormond. Another in 1572 refers to the Earl of Ormond's orchard 'being to the east from New Street'. Finally in 1583 the 'earl Thomas annexed a garden and tenement etc.,' 'to his great house at Carrickmacgriffin'. The later two probably relate to the extension and laying out of the Earl's park and gardens during those years.

During the 1640s Ormond Castle was used for meetings of 'The Confederation of Kilkenny', the Catholic alliance between leaders of the Old Irish and Old English groups. Owen Roe O'Neill wrote to a relative of the Earl's in 1644 that 'we have a provincial meeting this day at Carrick'. Five years later the castle was attacked by the Cromwellian army, captured and granted to a Commonwealth officer named Sir John Reynolds. Although there was no loss of life there are reports of severe damage to the fortifications. By 1660 the Duchess of Ormonde was writing to her agent, 'I understand by a letter from Ned Butler and others that the house at Carrick is in a ruinous condition.....' Some repairs were carried out and additions were made during the latter half of that century. At the end of the 18th century, contemporary drawings show the whole area between the north range and the river packed with buildings in varying stages of decay. Some of these buildings were said to have been demolished and further modernising additions made sometime after 1816 by a Mr. Wogan who was a tenant at the castle. Today very little remains in the enclosure to the south of the two towers.

Below: Kilkenny Castle from Windgap Hill, (detail) from a drawing by Francis Place (1647-1728) of c. 1690.

THE FORTIFIED CASTLE

The Towers

Although there is little evidence about the building of the two towers at Ormond Castle, it is clear that they were closely integrated into the building programme of Thomas Butler, 10th Earl of Ormond, and as such they should be included in any study of the castle.

Tower houses such as those at Ormond Castle were the commonest form of fortified house built in Ireland between the 15th and the mid 17th centuries. They often stood in a fortified bawn. It is likely that the bawn walls to the north of the towers were swept away to make room for building the new house in 1565. Ruined

towerhouses are to be found all over Ireland today. Many like those at Ormond Castle were added to at a later date and from the early part of 17th century; it was common to find stone houses adjoining these structures. The 10th Earl was also responsible for building a three storied range along the northern curtain wall between the two towers at Kilkenny castle. Several other examples of this practice are to be found at a later date at Lemanagh in Co. Clare, an O'Brien stronghold, where a four storied house with attic was constructed in the mid 17th century abutting an earlier tower built in 1500-1530. Other Butler properties, such as Dunmore House and Cloughgrenan Castle also conformed to this pattern. Defensive towerhouses were popular in Scotland as well and many of those have also been transformed by the addition of comfortable stone houses.

The Eastern Tower

The smaller tower c. 1450 on the eastern side is probably the earlier of the two towerhouses. It is five stories high and has been extensively altered over the centuries; blocked up doorways can be seen on three faces of this tower. The lowest floor is windowless (except for arrowloops) and is vaulted, the usual method of construction for stone buildings of the period. Staircases in this tower above the level of the north range are built into the thickness of the walls. The principal living quarters with fireplaces would have been on the upper floors. This particular tower contains an interesting arched structure which was inserted into the northern wall at fourth floor level. This could have been a great window, similar to the remaining example in the ruined great hall at Granagh. Both structures are deeply recessed and both have similar carved angels on either side of the

Above: eastern tower, view from south west. Closed doorways and the outline of high pitched roof can be seen.

Right: undercroft of eastern tower, showing fragments of wicker centering still adhering to the ceiling.

soffit. Later, during Earl Thomas's building programme, the abutting wall of the new north range blocked the ope. In order to integrate this tower into the overall design for his new house, large windows with stone mullions and hood mouldings were inserted into its eastern face. Illustrations of the eastern side of Ormond Castle in the 18th century show that a large building of at least three stories adjoined this tower to the south. The imprint of a pitched roofline suitable to this adjoining building and portions of rubble masonry can still be clearly seen adhering to the southern aspect of this tower from the lower courtyard beyond the gateway.

The Courtyard Doorway

In line with the principal entrance is a cut-stone doorway inserted into the opposite wall. The classical elements included in its design suggest a construction date in the 1560s, close to that of the north range. A small drawing sketched by Harold Leask from a map of 1699 would seem to indicate that this doorway was the central feature of a tall gabled building between the two towers. We also know from later drawings that a tall building did exist on this site and that beyond this gateway other ranges of building extended on both sides of the lower courtyard. It is not possible to ascertain exactly what type of buildings existed in this area during the 10th Earl's time. Those on the east would probably have held lodgings for guests and their retainers, while those to the west would have formed service areas ancillary to the great hall. Today all that remains in the enclosure south of the towers are just a few footings of earlier structures, some changes of level and the ruined three storeyed water gate standing starkly in the riverside wall, marooned by the dropping river receding over time.

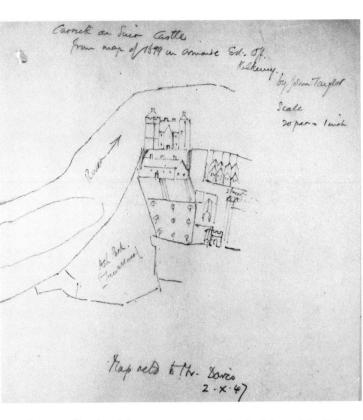

Above: sketch of Ormond Castle in 1699, by Harold Leask, taken from a map of that date by John Taylor. The sketch shows the north range as a low block in front of the taller building between the two towers. The town gate can be seen in the north west corner of the drawing.

Below: carved stone gateway in southern wall of the inner court.

Eighteenth century illustrations show a building of at least three storeys bridging the courtyard gateway area. The position of the gateway giving access to an inner court, which would have contained a great hall, follows the plan of early English courtyard houses. Such a layout of buildings does in fact fit the slim evidence remaining at Ormond Castle. The remnants of a great oriel window still exist in the western enclosing wall about thirty feet beyond the tower. Such an impressive window would be

Right: remains of oriel window, view from west.

Below: watergate, view from the lower court.

expected to light the dais end of a great hall and suggests that this large chamber abutted the western tower along the present perimeter wall south towards the river. At Kilkenny Castle the great hall was also situated to the right of the enclosure beyond the gatehouse.

The Western Tower

It seems probable that this second towerhouse was added on the western side of the enclosure at the end of the 15th century, while other buildings and alterations to the castle continued to be made during the early years of the 16th century. The second towerhouse is larger than the earlier one and has a rectangular projecting stair turret. Now in a ruined state, the eastern wall remained standing until 1903. Like the other tower, it has five storeys with remodelled windows. From the evidence of three impressive ruined fireplaces embedded in the southern wall and fragments of plasterwork (now vanished) known from old photographs, it can be established that this tower, like its companion, had an important role to play in the overall scheme of the 10th Earl's building programme during the latter part of the 16th century.

THE MANOR HOUSE/NORTH RANGE

Left: north range, view from park.

Below: view from east showing bay window and eastern tower.

Description

The north range consists of a long central block with two projecting wings joining it to the two towers, forming a half H-shaped building of two storeys with attic space. On the symmetrical northern front there are three bays to either side of a projecting central bay, which also contains the principal entrance. The house is just one room deep. The windows at ground floor level were originally much narrower for defensive purposes; these have since been carefully enlarged. Windows of the first floor are larger than those of either of the other floors, denoting the importance of the rooms on this level of the building. The attic storey is gabled and each of these contains a window to light that area. A parapet joining the gables runs all around the building. This was a common practice and can be seen in several coeval houses in England.

Both the eastern and western facades of the building also have three gables before they join with the towers. On the eastern facade there is another projecting bay, which has a large eleven-light window at first floor level, while on the western facade the central gable includes the projecting angled staircase turret.

The exterior of the building is very plain with hood mouldings on the windows and ornamental finials on the gables being the only decoration. All of the windows including those inserted in the two towers and remaining fragments of the western wall are of similar design with semi-elliptical arches and stone mullions, although they differ in size. A further unifying factor is a form of string course, portions of which still run above the first floor windows at roof level around the outerfacing walls of the house and both towers. The windows would have had small leaded panes of glass when they were first inserted. The main doorway and porch of the house are unusually stark and devoid of ornament.

Social Context

The enlargement of Ormond Castle by the addition of the north range was in keeping with the new and more comfortable living styles being adopted throughout Europe during the 16th century. In England the rise in living standards was due to flourishing trade as a result of thriving industry and agriculture. During the Elizabethan period, country houses were perceived as symbols of the owner's status which publicly demonstrated the prosperity, modernity and often the loyalty of their builders to the Queen.

Members of the Ormond family had for generations maintained strong and direct links with England and the Court and as we already know Thomas Butler had been educated and lived there throughout his formative years. He was a staunch supporter of three successive Tudor monarchs, Edward, Mary and Elizabeth and profited from this. Many honours and lucrative posts were bestowed on him by Queen Elizabeth and it is only natural that he should wish to emulate the style of living that he had experienced during his time in England. His father James, 9th Earl of Ormond, in his will referred to Ormond Castle at Carrick as one of his second best houses. So it should come as no surprise that the 10th Earl would wish to enhance this property which eventually was to become his favourite residence in Ireland.

The overall design of the north range was a commonplace one in England during the mid to late 16th century. Houses built in this way are still to be found in large numbers dotted all over the West Country in England. However, it is not the exterior of this building that is remarkable, rather the quality of the interior decoration. This is

*Left: Elizabeth I the 'Phoenix'
portrait by Nicholas Hilliard
(1547-1619), painted c.1572-6.*

outstanding and unique in this country; no other decorative scheme in Ireland
proclaims in plaster such a paean of praise and profession of loyalty to the Tudor
monarchy, particularly Queen Elizabeth, as that at Ormond Castle.

Below: Room 1 showing fireplace
with the Preston/Butler coat of
arms and date 1641.

DESIGN OF THE NORTH RANGE

We do not know who designed the north range at Ormond Castle, or who was
employed to build it. In England master masons were responsible for carrying out building works of this type and often drew up the plans as well. One such mason in England
is described in the record of his burial in 1599 as being, ' a very skilful man in the art of
masonry, in setting of plottes for buildings and performing the same ...as doth appear by
his works which may be seen etc...' The plan for Ormond Castle took the form of a
large detailed wooden model, described as 'The model of Carrick House' and listed in
an inventory taken in 1675 at Dunmore House, the favourite residence of Elizabeth (c.
1618-1684), 1st Duchess of Ormond. It is fitting that such a model should have been
preserved at Dunmore because Elizabeth was Thomas Butler's granddaughter and
heiress to most of the Butler lands through her mother Elizabeth Butler, Countess of
Desmond (d. 1628). Wooden scale models were used to demonstrate designs, rather
like architectural drawings of today. A great model of St Paul's Cathedral in London,
built during the later years of the 17th century for the eminent architect Sir
Christopher Wren, still exists today. The existence of a more mundane model 'of the
prison at Clonmel' for Sir William Robinson (c. 1643-1712) the architect is also known.
The model of Ormond Castle would seem to be the earliest known in these islands. A
model of Longleat House in England dated to 1567 was made by the French joiner

Adrian Gaunt who also worked on the building of that house. This cost £4.15s, and has until now been the first recorded example in England. Examples of the rates of pay at that time are also usefully recorded in the building records of Longleat where the principal masons were paid at a rate of 16 pence per day while the head carpenter was on the lower rate of 12 pence daily rate.

Although the north range is built of local stone and includes some Irish features in its construction, it is likely that the master mason was brought over from England by the 10th Earl to supervise and oversee the work. It may have taken up to ten years to complete. If we accept 1565 as the starting date and 1567 when supplies were to be delivered from Antwerp then the structure of the house must have been close to completion at that time. However the interior decoration, particularly that of the long gallery may have taken longer than expected. Decorative plasterwork was usually inserted before the floor boards were laid on the joists. The underfloors of several Elizabethan houses in England have yielded up samples of plasterwork fragments which had fallen in there during the decoration process. Only when the 'frets', as decorative plasterwork was referred to, were complete were wainscot and windows inserted into a building.

Above: the long gallery looking east.

The long gallery at Ormond Castle is remarkable for several reasons. Firstly it is the only example of its kind remaining in Ireland. Secondly it contains fine decorative plasterwork of a sophisticated nature. Finally and perhaps most striking is the subtlety of the actual layout of the gallery itself. The fenestration is arranged in a manner recommended in an architectural treatise published in France in 1561. In this work it is suggested that as the gallery is lit from both sides, windows are displaced so that each intervening portion of wall is bathed in light from the window opposite. Tall windows at each end of the gallery add even more to the overall lightness of the room. Another feature is the large recess formed by the projecting bay of the porch which is sited

immediately opposite the second fireplace in the gallery, allowing better access to a heat source in cold weather. Such recesses also served as viewing points for looking out at gardens and park in wet weather and are described in nostalgic fashion by the 17th century historian and writer on architecture, Roger North as also being useful for 'select companys to converse in.......being small withdrawing rooms to the grand tour of the gallery'.

Above: the recess in the long gallery where three shot holes can be seen.

FUNCTION

Because of its small size the north range at Carrick could not have functioned as a self-contained building. It was fully integrated with the two towerhouses and provided a suite of 'State Rooms' and fine lodgings decorated in the newest fashion for important visitors. This arrangement included the use of some of the older rooms in the earlier towers. Prior to the building of the new range, the hall and great chamber would have been the focal point of the principal rooms; long galleries being a fairly recent fashion. It is likely that an oriel window, the base of which can still be seen in the ruined west wall, lit the dais end of such a great hall. It is also probable that the old great chamber was housed on the first floor of the western tower, so that when the north range was built, a way through from the towers was made to enlarge the accommodation potential of the house and to facilitate circulation. It may be that the building which existed over the central doorway was also part of the 10th Earl's building programme. Such an arrangement would have greatly aided circulation and would have enclosed the inner court in a symmetrical fashion.

As it was usual to approach the principal rooms (State Rooms) up an imposing staircase, it is possible that entrance was made to these rooms from the great hall end. Given the relative magnificence of the State Rooms at Ormond Castle, the modest staircase (rebuilt) enclosed in its own tower does not seem to come up to standard. However it may be that a new grand staircase was housed in the problematic building between the two towers.

Decorative Plasterwork at Ormond Castle

The decorative plasterwork in this building is of considerable interest, providing as it does the finest early examples of this medium to be found in Ireland. The forms of plaster decoration used in the friezes in the two principal rooms, the long gallery and the Earl's Chamber at Ormond Castle, are Flemish in style. This is not surprising as Antwerp was the most important centre for commercial and cultural exchange in Europe at this time. Flemish influence in the arts was disseminated by the use of illustrated pattern books which were widely circulated. Many books of this type containing illustrations of Italian and Renaissance Mannerist ornament as interpreted by the Antwerp engravers reached England where they were eagerly accepted. This new fashion for strapwork and Italian *grottesche* was initially used on interiors but soon became

Above: detail of ornamental frieze and decorated ceiling from long gallery.

Above: detail of ornamental frieze, showing strapwork cartouche from the Earl's chamber.

common as decorative features on the exteriors of many great Elizabethan houses. On the great carved wooden screen at Middle Temple Hall in London, which probably dates from 1562-70, for example, can be seen arrangements of allegorical figures in shell niches flanked by fluted ionic pilasters similar to those in the two principal rooms at Ormond Castle; other ornamental elements such as those used on the strapwork cartouches in the Ormond decorative plasterwork are also present on the screen.

Further confirmation of the Flemish connection can be gathered from the fact that the wainscot panelling and glass for Ormond Castle had been ordered from Antwerp in 1566 through the offices of Sir Thomas Gresham (1519-79), a wealthy merchant who was also Royal Agent for three Tudor monarchs. In the 1560s Gresham was not only building a courtyard house for himself at Bishopsgate in London but also, significantly, in 1566 was involved in constructing a London Exchange for merchants in which Flemish bricklayers and other craftsmen were employed. Such usage of craftsmen from abroad was not new. Earlier in the century they had been employed in large numbers by that great royal builder King Henry VIII. It is likely then that Flemish workers either came directly from Antwerp or were hired from London to carry out decoration at Ormond Castle.

General ornament in the plasterwork and some specific decorative motifs such as the lion masks or the small elf-like figures astride some of the cartouches can be linked to a series of books of grotesque designs for decoration by Jan Vreedman de Vries, published in Antwerp. One of these books entitled *Grottesco: in diversche manieren,* dated 1565, was specifically aimed at artists, glasscutters and various other craftsmen, who wished to carry out their decoration in the 'Antique Manner'. Earlier works on the same subject were also published in Antwerp but de Vries seems to have proved the most popular author in this field at that particular time. Therefore we can appreciate that the decoration at Ormond Castle was absolutely up to date and carried out using the most fashionable motifs of the day. Photographs taken during the most recent restoration when the surviving plasterwork was cleaned down prior to taking moulds, confirm that the quality of the workmanship was of the highest standard.

The use of the roundel as a framing device for the Royal arms and portraits in the long gallery was a fashion that had originated in Italy and spread to England during the reign of Henry VIII. It may have derived from the 16th century popularity of portraits taken from antique coins. Cardinal Wolsey employed the Italian artist Giovanni da

DECORATIVE PLASTERWORK

Maiano to make a series of painted and gilded terracotta roundels for his great palace at Hampton Court. In the frieze in the long gallery at Ormond Castle, roundels frame plaster portraits of Queen Elizabeth I, her brother, King Edward VI and the Tudor Royal arms. These plasterwork portraits are skilfully executed in crisply modelled high relief, as are the strapwork cartouches. Their exquisite costume details would indicate a date between 1565 and 1575, although by that time Edward had been dead for almost twenty years. Elizabeth is depicted with a small crown on her head and a sceptre leaning against her right shoulder. A portrait of the Queen by the Flemish artist Steven van der Meulen (fl. 1543-68) could be the source, for, although the Flemish portrait is an uncrowned image, it shares several costume features with the plaster one, such as the style of the neck ruff rising up from the gauzy neckline; the line of the stiff jewel-embossed bodice; the sleeve detail; the dressing of the hair and the ornamental snood. The van der Meulen portrait is also of the correct date and may have served as the model for an engraving of a portrait of Queen Elizabeth by Remigius Hogenberg c. 1570 which has strong similarities to the Ormond version.

The ceiling decoration at Ormond Castle would also indicate the period 1565-1575. The plain moulded geometric designs are very similar to those found at Sizeragh Castle

Above: portrait of Queen Elizabeth I, engraving by Remigius Hogenberg c. 1570. This engraved portrait is close to the portrait of the Queen by Steven van der Meulen (fl.1543-68). The head and costume details are close to the plaster portraits at Ormond Castle.

Left: detail of ornamental frieze, showing portrait of Elizabeth I in roundel from the long gallery.

in Cumbria, a building of approximately the same date. The plain plaster mouldings are a direct development from an earlier method in which wooden batons were used to decorate flat plaster ceilings with similar patterns. Another example of this type of translation from wood to plaster can be seen in the pendants of the long gallery ceiling. Later forms of plasterwork move away from the geometric and towards a more curvilinear style which featured flowers and other naturalistic details. Examples of this later type of plasterwork can be seen at Bunratty Castle in Co. Clare 1610-20 and in the long galleries at Knole in Kent (1603-8) and Powis Castle in Wales (1587-96).

The heraldic details of the decorative schemes were probably painted, primary colours and gilding being the most commonly used to highlight armorial devices. It may be that the plasterwork frieze in the long gallery was also gilded, although it was common enough to leave this type of decoration unpainted to create a marble effect. No other examples of decorative plasterwork of a comparative standard from this period have survived in Ireland. Later examples dating from the early 17th century seem coarser and lacking in sophistication in both design and execution.

WHEN IN RESIDENCE, Thomas Butler, 10th Earl of Ormond, a powerful owner of land and property, undoubtedly had a large household of up to a hundred retainers and servants lodged on the premises. His early upbringing at the English Court probably meant that life at Ormond Castle was organised along similar lines. Mark Girouard's description of life at Hardwick House in Derbyshire as 'a grand Elizabethan household ... organised like a little court' was true for such a great landowner in Ireland as in England.

In the Ormond papers the only information found to date about servants at Ormond Castle is a brief mention of a proctor and an attorney, both upper servants involved in estate management, in the household of Piers, the 8th Earl. Staff were usually men; women were employed only in a few very specific areas, for example, as personal maids and nurses for the children, while gentlewomen served mainly as companions and assistants to the lady of the house. In the 16th century men from the lower ranks carried out most of the heavy work in both house and kitchens. They were also employed to work in the stables and in the park around the castle. In such large households strictly defined divisions also existed between upper and lower servants.

Divisions between family and servants in the 16th century were often underlined by the quality of their lodgings and where they dined. Upper servants, whose responsibilities included running the estate and the stables as well as the household, were usually members of the landed classes themselves and were often young as they were taken into great houses as part of their training for future life; they were considered as gentlemen and gentlewomen and addressed as 'Mr.' or 'Mrs'. Together with proctors, attorneys and clergymen attached to the household, they all had reasonable accommodation by the standards of the day, but lower servants such as grooms, kitchen staff and others would sleep under tables, in pantries, stable buildings, attics, or wherever they could find space to lay their heads. Upper servants, particularly the gentlewomen, had the use of some of the smaller parlours and these rooms were often referred to as 'the gentlewomen's eating parlour'. Lower servants ate in the hall, where visiting servants often joined them during the day when they were not occupied with other tasks, to gossip and while away the time.

Even though Elizabethan households were formal in their organisation and extensive regulations existed to ensure their smooth running, it was not the rigidly segregated form that became the norm by the 19th century. Rooms in most instances served two or more purposes. The entrance hall through which important visitors made their way also served as the servants' hall. Tables could be set up anywhere for eating and business could be conducted in any one of several rooms. According to Girouard, 'Houses

THE HOUSEHOLD AT ORMOND CASTLE

Above: a tudor rose in low relief lies above a cable roll at the angle of the stop-chamfer on each jamb of a doorway in a building west of the castle.

were divided not according to function, with living rooms below and bedrooms above, but according to state; on each floor the rooms grew more cere-monial'. The most important room in the house would have been the great chamber which had by Elizabethan times taken over from the great hall as the place where the owner dined in state. It was always the most richly decorated room and often contained the Royal coat of arms as a symbol of the owner's loyalty.

By modern standards life in a great house like Ormond Castle would have been fairly uncomfortable: damp was pervasive; all cooking and heating was by open fires, with brick ovens for baking; lighting was by candles. Water may have been brought into the house by a primitive pumping device, but sanitary facilities would have been very basic.

OUTBUILDINGS

We know that during the 17th century there were several ranges of outbuildings at Ormond Castle, many of which probably dated from earlier times. Stables were required for the large number of horses used by such a household, while the brewhouses common to large households in those days would have been sited down near the river. Early ord-nance survey maps show the existence of a 'Lodge' or small house, on the southernmost corner of the eastern park wall, within easy walking distance of the main house. Formal garden patterns can also be discerned on the same maps, to the north east of the Lodge. Lodges, usually tall structures, often built on the edge of the park, were a notable feature of late Elizabethan living; they were often used both as a viewing point for overlooking the park and as a 'banqueting house' where light meals or 'sweets' were served. A most elegant later example was the classical style, circular 'banqueting house' which existed at Kilkenny Castle during the 17th century.

GARDENS

The remains of a walled garden still exist to the east of the castle. In this garden area there are remnants of a two storied 16th century building. Carefully incised Tudor roses with a small rope moulding can been seen at the base of each door pillar. The window openings all have hood mouldings. A garden such as this, close to the castle and with direct access from the house would have been used as a privy or private garden by the family. This is where Thomas Butler might have strolled with only his closest family or acquaintances for company. Peaches were grown in special peach houses at Ormond Castle during the 17th century and there were also extensive orchards on the lands bordering on New Street, although, it has not been possible to pinpoint a site.

THE RESTORATION WORK AT ORMOND CASTLE

Right: old photograph (1907) showing panelling in situ in the Earl's Chamber before its removal to Kilkenny Castle.

Below: two of the Ormond badges, that on the left showing the Butler coat of arms, on the right the 10th Earl's personal badge with the letters T O, Thomas Ormond.

Ormond Castle, Carrick-on-Suir

THE CASTLE WAS PLACED in OPW guardianship in 1947 (it was later taken into state own-ership). Shortly after, conservation work started with clearing of the courtyard, removal of ivy from the front and side of the building. Concrete lintels were put in, in the rooms on the upper level. Restoration work included new floors and windows, and roof repairs. The southeast tower was roofed in 1949. A concrete spiral stairs was put in the north-west tower. During the course of works, wood-beetle (*anobium paretatum*) was found in the roof timbers and this was treated. In 1951, the lower courtyard was

excavated and a retaining wall was built. Evidence of an original parapet wall at roof level was found (sprockets were added to the rafters). In 1952 the limestone fireplace which had been removed from the castle to Kilkenny Castle was returned to Carrick and reinstated in the long gallery.

In 1958 the chimneys were dismantled and restored. A temporary roof was built over the original roof to allow roof repairs to be carried out. The trusses and rafters were taken down, the parapets restored and the roof repaired with minor replacement of original timbers. A new oak floor was

laid in the attic space. This work took about 2 years. At this time some of the plasterwork was taken down and stored, with the intention of restoration but this was not done then. In 1982, the floor in the long gallery was renewed. In 1985, floors were inserted in the southeast tower and a stairs fitted. Fire and intruder alarms were installed.

Plaster restoration commenced in 1985. The project was carried out in conjunction with AnCO (FÁS as it is now) in Galway, who organised a plaster moulding course in conjunction with OPW. In-situ plaster was repaired and refixed. Casts were taken of original plaster motifs and panels and the ceilings and friezes in the long gallery and the other two rooms on first floor level were restored. The friezes were almost intact in the two small rooms and the ceilings were based on photographs which showed parts of the original ceiling in one case and typical mouldings only in the case of the room at the top of the stairs. In the long gallery, enough of the original ceiling existed in-situ or was recorded in drawings to allow for accurate completion of the ceiling. The pattern of the friezes was evident and the infill panels were made from the casts of the original examples.

In the long gallery, the limestone fireplace that had been transferred back from Kilkenny Castle, was reset at the correct level (it had been set too low, to suit the floor level at the time). The main rooms in the castle have been furnished with 16th and 17th century furniture. Conservation work has been carried out to the southwest tower.

The castle is no longer used as living quarters for the caretaker and the ground floor rooms have been adapted for use as a visitor reception room, toilets and guide facilities and two exhibition areas. One of the exhibition rooms houses a display of charters which relate to the Butler family. These were kindly lent to the castle by the late Mr. Hubert Butler.

Today, access to the attic space allows the visitor to inspect and appreciate the intricate structure of the timber structures supporting the roof.

Left: plasterwork before restoration.

Below: roof under repair in the 1950's. The temporary roof allowed restoration of the parapets and treatment of the timber.

Written by Jane Fenlon
Co-ordinator: Aighleann O'Shaughnessy
Design: John Power
Photography: Con Brogan
Origination: Colour Repro
Printed by: Nicholson & Bass

An **Roinn Ealaíon, Cultúir 7 Gaeltachta**
Department of Arts, Culture and the Gaeltacht

Oifig na nOibreacha Poiblí
The Office of Public Works

Acknowledgements

The National Monuments and Historic Properties Service and the author would like to thank the following for their assistance in the preparation of this booklet:
Elizabeth Mayes, Edward McParland, Zoe Devlin, Claire Gapper, London,
The Chief Herald and staff of the Genealogical Office Dublin.

All illustrations, unless otherwise stated, from the Office of Public Works.

• James Butler, (d. 1546), 9th Earl of Ormond, drawing by Hans Holbein the younger (1497/8-1543).
  The Royal Collection H.M. Queen Elizabeth II (page 18).
• Thomas Butler, (1531-1614), 10th Earl of Ormond, portrait, oil on panel by unknown artist.
  Harris Museum & Art Gallery, Preston England (page 19).
• Capture of Thomas Earl of Ormond by O'More 1600. *Reproduced with permission of The Board of*
  Trinity College Dublin (page 20).
• Rubbing of coat of arms. *Grainne Carr (page 21)* .
• James Butler, (1610-1688), 12th Earl of Ormond.
  Philadelphia Museum of Art, Philadelphia USA, bequest of Arthur H. Lea (page 21).
• James Butler, (1665-1745) 2nd Duke of Ormonde. *Courtesy Historical Portraits Ltd., London (page 24).*
• Ormond Castle, drawing signed Purcell Pinxit, 1782. *National Library of Ireland (page 25).*
• Ormond Castle, Aquatint, artist Thomas Sautelle Roberts, (1760-1826). *National Library of Ireland (page 27).*
• Granagh Castle, Co. Kilkenny. *Victoria and Albert Museum, London (page 28).*
• Kilkenny Castle from Windgap Hill. *National Gallery of Ireland (page 29).*
• Elizabeth I the 'Phoenix' portrait by Nicholas Hilliard (1547-1619). *National Portrait Gallery London (page 35).*
• Portrait of Elizabeth I, engraving by Remigius Hogenberg c. 1570. *Prints and Drawing Dept.,*
  British Museum, London (page 41).
• Birr Castle, Co. Offaly. *Birr Scientific & Heritage Foundation (page 42).*
• Family tree: *Grainne Carr*

Published by Stationery Office. To be purchased through any bookseller, or directly from the
Government Publications Sale Office, Sun Alliance House, Molesworth Street, Dublin 2.
ISBN: 0-7076-2400-2
© 1996 Government of Ireland

Sources

There is no single source for the buildings at Ormond Castle, Carrick on Suir. The main sources used were documents, letters and deeds from the Ormond family papers contained mainly in the *Ormonde MSS, Calendar of the Manuscripts of the Marquess of Ormonde, preserved at Kilkenny Castle* (H.M.C. 11 vols, London), the *Ormond Deeds 1172-1350* (I.M.C., 6 vols, Dublin) and the collection of original Ormonde MS in the National Library of Ireland. *The Castle and Manor House at Carrick on Suir, Co. Tipperary* an unpublished BA Thesis TCD by Frances D. Nowlan also provided useful information. Various reports on Ormond Castle by H. G. Leask, when Inspector of National Monuments Board of Works, were consulted (MS OPW and National Archives, Dublin).